T0103726

7 STEPS FOR AN EFFECTUAL PRAYER

7 STEPS FOR AN EFFECTUAL PRAYER

JOSEPH T. DOSSO

authorHOUSE®

AuthorHouse™ UK Ltd.
1663 Liberty Drive
Bloomington, IN 47403 USA
www.authorhouse.co.uk
Phone: 0800.197.4150

© *2014 Joseph T. Dosso. All rights reserved.*

No part of this book may be reproduced, stored in a retrieval system, or transmitted by any means without the written permission of the author.

Scripture quotations marked KJV are from the Holy Bible, King James Version (Authorized Version). First published in 1611. Quoted from the KJV Classic Reference Bible, Copyright © *1983 by The Zondervan Corporation.*

Published by AuthorHouse 07/07/2014

ISBN: 978-1-4969-8599-6 (sc)
ISBN: 978-1-4969-8600-9 (hc)
ISBN: 978-1-4969-8601-6 (e)

Any people depicted in stock imagery provided by Thinkstock are models, and such images are being used for illustrative purposes only. Certain stock imagery © *Thinkstock.*

This book is printed on acid-free paper.

Because of the dynamic nature of the Internet, any web addresses or links contained in this book may have changed since publication and may no longer be valid. The views expressed in this work are solely those of the author and do not necessarily reflect the views of the publisher, and the publisher hereby disclaims any responsibility for them.

DEDICATE

I would like to dedicate this book to the Holy Spirit of the living God, for inspiring me in writing this book on prayer which is a mighty weapon of Spiritual warfare in the hands of believers.

CONTENTS

ACKNOWLEDGEMENTS

God in his infinite grace has made it possible for his revelation on prayer to be made available for the edification and building of the body of Christ. I would like to extend my personal thank you to the following persons that have been instrumental to the printing out of this book:

Claize M. Dosso, Joshua Ngongo, Florance Cerutti, Venance Kouassi, Zephirain Horinth, Seiwa Cunningham, Philroy Forte, Sister Clarice.

FOREWORD
BY BISHOP Al BAXTER

In his book on prayer, Pastor Joseph Dosso deals with principles in praying and getting result. This subject lays at the very heart of the Christian daily life and yet many Christian neglect praying because it demands a fundamental reality and a knowing that we are in dialogue with the unseen Supreme Being. Pastor Joseph provides us with extremely useful tools and practical guidance to help real people in the real world who yearn to be in a higher dimension of spiritual collaboration and communication with God. A practice of these simple but effective and practical principles will guarantee that a year from now your life will be better than it has ever been.

With this book Pastor Joseph ignites the fire within you and lights the path to spiritual success. This book presents us with a serious challenge to examine our prayer life in terms of how to pray, when to pray and what to pray

INTRODUCTION

The Christian faith is based on our relationship with the Almighty Jehovah God. A relationship is a fellowship: a communion existing between two persons. The beauty of any relationship is revealed or consolidated by the act of communication between the parties involved. Communication is the sharing of information. The act of communication is only established when the **"speaking"** and **"listening"** element are in place.

Communication between man and God is qualified as 'prayer'. If prayer is considered to be an act of communication therefore, it has to have the *speaking* and *listening* aspects to it.

Prayer is not only an act or a way of *requesting* things from God, but also the essential method of communication between us and God.

I would like you to understand that prayer is not only speaking to God, but it is also *hearing* from Him.

Any time we go in prayer before God, but fail to take time to hear from Him, we have positioned ourselves to be frustrated. Today, in the body of Christ, we can see great frustrations in the lives of many Christians. We may ask why? It is because of this important fact of waiting to hear back from Him. You can't make the most out of something until you have the correct perspective of it or an adequate knowledge of it.

God is more eager to speak with you than you think. One thing is true: once this element is understood, your prayers will command authority and results.

There are some specific steps that need to be observed or followed in order for your prayer to command dominion from above. I am convinced that the disciples could see the differences between their prayers and Jesus', by the results Jesus' prayers commanded. That is the reason why they went and ask him to teach them how to pray.

Not only did they notice the difference in the results, but they also appreciated the place of prayer in their Christian walk. You will remain a victim in the hand of the pretender (devil), until you are totally committed in your prayer room.

Those that chose to live a prayerless life will never experience tangible victory down here on earth, even though they are set for heaven. They won't be able to enjoy the full package of redemption.

My friend, prayer is essential in your life and in mine. Even Jesus, who was God, showed us his addiction to prayer. The Bible says:

Luke 5:16 *"And he withdrew himself into the wilderness, and prayed."*

Luke 4:42 *"And when it was day, he departed and went into a desert place…"*

Luke 6:12 *"And it came to pass in those days, that he went out into a mountain to pray, and continued all night in prayer to God."*

Mark 1:35 *"… He went out, and departed into a solitary place, and there prayed."*

Mark 6:46 *"And when he had sent them away, he departed into a mountain to pray."*

Matthew 14:23 *"And when he had sent the multitudes away, he went up into a mountain apart to pray: and when the evening was come, he was there alone."*

All through these scriptures, it is clear that prayer occupied a great place in Jesus' life. In the next lines, we are going to study the required steps we need to follow according to Jesus' teaching, and how to hear from him in order to receive great prayer results.

CHAPTER 1

7 STEPS FOR AN EFFECTUAL PRAYER

As I said earlier, the disciples noticed the difference in the results that they achieved when praying. They then decided to go to the master so that he could teach them how to obtain the same results.

My brother, my sister, it is your knowledge of what to do and how to do it, that will guarantee your mastery over the issues in your life. Look at Jesus in the book of John, Chapter 6 - he was confronted with the fact that he had to feed the multitude. The disciples began to panic. Some suggested that they should send the multitudes back. Something very interesting strikes me about this scripture: it is the quiet and relaxed attitude that the Lord Jesus had. All through the scriptures, he never displays any stress.

The question that we need to ask ourselves is: "Why?" The answer to this question is in verse 6 of the sixth chapter of John (John 6:6): *"And this he said to prove him (Philip); for he himself knew what he would do."* When Jesus did what he needed to, the miraculous happened.

After some intensive study on the Lord's Prayer - "Our father who art in heaven" - I have discovered that this prayer, is instructional, a formula, rather than a prayer that needs to be repeated verbatim.

Let us examine Jesus' instruction for prayer according to Matthew Chapter 6 verse 9, (Matthew 6:9): ***"After this manner therefore pray ye…"***

Step 1: ACKNOWLEDGE HIM

In Matthew 6:9 the bible says: **"Our father which art in heaven, hallowed be your name"**

In the first words of this verse, the Lord Jesus is teaching us to acknowledge the supremacy of God.

That sentence *"Our Father which art in HEAVEN"*, reveals the greatness of God. The Lord Jesus is making us aware of the fact that we are praying to a God that is not from here, but from above. In other words, he wants us to be conscious of the fact that He is highly lifted up.

The second part of the verse says: *"Hallowed be thy name"*. In order for us to gain a full understanding of this part, it is important to first define the key word which is HALLOWED.

The American Heritage Dictionary defines 'HALLOWED' as, *"sanctified; consecrated; highly venerated; sacrosanct"*. To hallow is "to make or set apart as holy. To respect or honour greatly; revere." In simpler terms, we use 'hallowed' to refer to someone whom we should treat with awe and respect, because they deserve it.

This first step represents therefore acknowledging God for who he is. Worship Him for His person. It is vital for us to understand this very first step. You cannot start your prayer to the Father, without first recognising his majesty.

The Lord Jesus clearly said in his first words, *"Our Father who art in heaven"*. This plainly shows that Jesus is telling Him (the Father in heaven) "I am aware that you are not from here, but you are highly lifted up above the earth." Exalting God is the prerequisite if we would like to stand a chance of having our prayer answered. This is what we call worship.

Taking the time to exalt God at the very beginning of your prayer, is telling Him that "you do not pray only for what you can get from him, but rather for who he is."

Many of us do this in the natural. I remember when I was fourteen or fifteen years of age, whenever I wanted something special from my father (my biological father), I would tell him how remarkable, good, wonderful and kind he was that there was no one like him. That he was the best daddy that any kid would ever want to have. I would tell him that all my friends wished to have him as a father. At the end of all 'speech', came my request. Fortunately for me, it always worked!

Remember that we are all made in the image of God, therefore, I personally believe that this is the principle that the Lord Jesus Christ was teaching his disciples.

Understand that our heavenly father likes to be glorified. No wonder He said in Isaiah 42:8: *"I am the Lord: that is my name: and my glory will I not GIVE to another, neither my praise to graven images."*

I have come across many people that say, "God himself knows that I don't and will never take His glory." But the truth of the matter is that any time you fail to voice it, you have just taken His glory or despise His person. Never assume, but always make sure that you have given it to Him.

David said in Psalm 69:30: *"I will…magnify him…."*

I want you to know that worship is what ushers us into the presence of God so that our prayers might be heard and answered. Worship consists of acknowledging God for who HE IS rather than what He has done for us. I pray that today you will graduate to the level of a true worshiper. Your worship prepares the ground for your request. Stop starting your prayer with tears, just worship.

If God could have a need, it would be a need for worship. The Bible tells us in John 4:23: **"Yet a time is coming and has now come, when the true worshipers will WORSHIP the Father in spirit and in truth, for they are the kind of worshipers the Father SEEKS."**

We need to understand this fact very well. Worship gladdens the heart of God. It is therefore wisdom for us to approach Him with it.

Step 2: GIVE THANKS FOR HIS HAND UPON YOU

Matt 6:10 *"...Thy will be done in earth, as it is in heaven."*

What is the will of God concerning us? Jeremiah 29: 11 says, *"For I know the thoughts that I think towards you (my will for you), thoughts of peace, and not of evil, to give you an expected end."*

And 3 John 2 also says, *"Beloved, I wish above all things that thou mayest prosper and be in health, even as thy soul prospereth."*

These two scriptures help us to understand the will of God. They expose the mind of God concerning us. This understanding leads us to the fact that the second thing to consider in guaranteeing an answer to our prayers, is thanking God for His will in our life. The fact of you and I being alive, makes God worthy of our praise. We cannot open the windows of heaven with an attitude of ingratitude. Acknowledging God for what he has done for you so far, pushes Him to do what He has not yet done.

The Bible says in Psalm 100:4: *"Enter into his gates with thanksgiving and into his courts with praise; be thankful unto him and bless his name."*

Thanksgiving is a very important element if we would like to stand a chance of having our prayers answered. This is what helps us to go through the gates of heaven. Try to imagine that you are given an appointment for a job interview. Instead of following the normal protocol, which is coming to the meeting room through the main door, you decide to go to the room by the window. What are the chances of you getting that job? Probably zero. Why? It is not about someone being against you or something, but about the protocol not being respected. Friend, take time to give Him thanks. Appreciate God for all that He has done and are still doing for you. If it wasn't for Him, you wouldn't be here today. What are the values of the things that are stressing you out right now, compared to the breath of life that you have?

Even if things seem not to be working in your life, thank Him at least, that you are in good health. Thank Him that you were not a victim of ritual killers or of a road traffic accident. 1st Thessalonians, Chapter 5, verse 18, says *"In everything give thanks: for this is the will of God in Christ Jesus concerning you."*

Listen, what appears negative today, won't remain forever. It is the atmosphere of thanksgiving that you create, that secures your entrance into the tabernacle of answered prayer.

If there is one mistake that we need to avoid, it is to enter our prayer room with an ungrateful spirit. A spirit full of murmuring. Remember, things could have been worse, but by his mercy they are not so. The Apostle Paul insists on this fact in Ephesians 5: 20: *"Giving thanks always for all things unto God the father…"*

God is never pleased with complainers. We need to know that our God has never failed, neither can He ever fail. He takes great pleasure in the lives of those who constantly give Him all the glory. God will go to great lengths just to preserve His glory in your life. Isaiah 48:11 says: *"For mine own sake, even for mine own sake, will I do it: for how would my name be polluted? And I will not give my glory unto another."*

In this scripture, God is saying: "I will never allow any source of my glory to be polluted, corrupted or abandoned.

Whatsoever it takes to defend it and preserve it, I will do it." The time has come for us to graduate from the 'school of mourners and complainers', to 'the school of thanks givers'. This second step is very important in order for us to attract God's attention. Remember, you do not secure God's attention with your tears, only with your praise. This is so true, that even in the natural; you are attracted to the people that are always grateful and thankful to you. When Jesus healed the ten lepers, only one came back to say thank you. Fortunately for him, he was the only one that was also made whole. The favourable answer to your petition starts here. The same way as giving ushers in abundance, so is thanksgiving and praise, to the world of constant answered prayer. From today, become addicted to giving God thanks always for everything around your life, in Jesus precious name. Everything happens for a reason. God is always right, therefore He deserve to be praised. I like the way King David says it in Psalm 103: 1-2: *"Bless the Lord, O my soul: and all that is within me, bless his holy name. Bless the Lord, O my soul, and FORGET NOT all HIS BENEFITS."*

Step 3: PRESENT YOUR REQUEST

Matthew 6:11: *"GIVE us this day our daily bread."*

This is an important point for us to understand. Jesus is telling us to ask the Father for our daily bread, our salvation (from the Greek SOTERIA, meaning deliverance, restoration, empowerment, promotion, etc).

Asking things from God is your right as a son or daughter of God. You only receive what you ask for. Even in the natural, nothing will ever land in your lap until you ask for it. It is not a sign of humility or holiness NOT to ask from God. I have heard so many people say, "I am not going to ask, because God himself knows my needs and my problems." It is true that God knows your needs and appreciates what you are going through, but that won't change what He said in Matthew 7:7 *"ASK, and it shall be given you…."* **In other words, "DON'T ask, and it shall NOT be given unto you."**

In James 1:5, The Bible says, *"If any of you LACKS…, he should ASK God, who gives generously to all without finding fault, and it will be given to him"* (New International Version).

This scripture blew my mind the day I discovered it. The spirit of the Lord spoke into my heart there and then saying: asking and receiving is automatic. When you realise that you lack something, you should ASK for it to the one (God) who gives without question. It is one thing for you to know that you lack, but it is another thing for you to ask.

We need to drop that religious mentality that tells us not to ask things from God, for He Himself knows, and at the appointed time, He will do it. The Lord Jesus said in Chapter 21 verses 22 of the gospel of Saint Matthew: *"And all things, whatsoever ye shall ASK in prayer, believe, ye shall receive."* He went on repeating the same thing in Mark 11:24 *"Therefore I tell you, whatsoever you ASK for in prayer, believe that you have received it, and it will be yours."* (NIV)

And

Luke 11:9 *"And I say unto you, ASK, and it shall be given you..."* (KJV)

The person that fascinates me as far as ASKING is concerned is Martha, Lazarus' sister. She acknowledged the fact that it was over in the natural, as stated in John 11:21 *"then said Martha unto Jesus, Lord, if thou hadst been here, my brother had not died."* However, she knew deep inside of her that there was still a way out of this situation. She said in verse 22, **"BUT I KNOW, *that even now, whatsoever thou wilt ASK of God, God will give it thee."***

I pray that you may embrace this truth. Heaven is just waiting to hear from you. All the angelic hosts and forces are already set by God for the despatching of your answers. Remember that God's desire is for us to have good and pleasant things that contribute to our godliness. Paul in Ephesians 3:20, tells us of the awesomeness of God's divine power that works in us. The interesting thing in this scripture is that all that God can do depends on what we ASK. Look at what is written: *"Now unto him that is able to do exceeding abundantly above all that we ASK or think, according to the power that worketh in us."* My brother and my sister let us get busy ASKING according to his will.

You can come out of that situation today if only you ASK your heavenly father. You don't have to die where you are today. That sickness can leave you today, just ASK. Stop complaining about life, but start ASKING God to fill up your life. I believe that God won't give you what you haven't asked for, so that it may not look forced on you, as said in

Philemon 14: *"But without thy mind would I do nothing; that thy benefit should not be as it were of necessity, but willingly."*

I pray that God may grant you the grace to ask in the name of Jesus Christ.

Step 4: DEFEND AND PRESENT YOUR STRONG REASON

Matthew 6:12 *"And forgive us our debts, as we forgive our debtors."*

This scripture has always confused people. We know that confusion leads to destruction. This is also true in the spiritual.

In this scripture, the Lord Jesus was not talking about asking forgiveness at the time of prayer, but rather praying with the word of God, in other words, reminding God of what He has said.

The reason this revelation is true is this: How many times a day do you pray? Let's say you pray three times a day: morning, noon and night, before going to bed. Try to imagine that after your noon prayer you miss your way again, in the sense that you sin against God. Would you wait till the evening to ask for forgiveness? If you have to wait for the evening prayer to repent of that sin, that means you may miss heaven if Jesus comes back before the time of your evening prayer!

Let me make a clear note here, I believe in and practice the asking of forgiveness of sin. This should be done at the time when we realise that we have missed our way, not only at a set time of prayer or when we feel low. Otherwise you will develop a constant feeling of guilt. This habit has made many Christian walk with a victim mentality; always feeling unworthy of God's presence.

If you are truly born again, remember that you are no longer under the power of sin, therefore the Lord expects you to live above sin. The Bible says in 1John 3:9 (Amp) *"No one born (begotten) of God [deliberately, knowingly and habitually] practices sin, for God's nature abides in him [His principle of life, the divine sperm, remains permanently within him]; and he cannot practice sinning because he is born (begotten) of God."* Further down in Chapter 5, verses 4 to 5 the scriptures confirm the same thing: *"For whatever is born of God is victorious over the world (sin); and this is the victory that conquers the world (sin), even our faith. Who is it that is victorious over (that conquers] the world (sin) but he who believes that Jesus is the son of God [who adheres to, trust in, and relies on that fact]"*. (Amp)

The understanding of this point is crucial, so that we may avoid labouring in vain in our prayer room. It is not the fact of asking for forgiveness that determines your access to the throne of God, but rather, it is your righteousness that determines it. Righteousness is not determined by works, but by faith. That is why Paul said in Galatians 2:21 (AMP) *"[Therefore, I do not treat God's gracious gift as something of minor importance and defeat its very purpose]; I do not set aside and invalidate and frustrate and nullify the grace (unmerited favour) of God. For if justification (righteousness, acquittal from guilt) comes through [observing the ritual of] the law, then Christ (the Messiah) died groundlessly and to no purpose and in vain. [His death was then wholly superfluous]."*

Your righteousness depends on your faith. When you believe in your heart that Christ came and died for you, you automatically become righteous in the sight of God. Because He no longer sees you directly, but He sees you through the blood of Jesus Christ, that establishes your redemption. God declared in Isaiah 54:17: *"...and their righteousness is of me, saith the Lord."* The Bible testifies that the righteousness of Abraham was of faith in Romans 4:3 *"For what saith the scripture? Abraham BELIEVED God, and it was counted unto him for righteousness."* (KJV)

God reinforces this fact in Romans 3: 27 to 28: **"Where is boasting then? It is excluded. By what law? Of works? Nay: but by the law of Faith. Therefore we conclude that a man is justified by Faith without the deeds of the law."**

Beloved, let this truth sink into your conscience so that the devil may lose any grip of condemnation that he has placed over your life, your family and anything that belongs to you.

As mentioned above, the instruction of Jesus is to pray according to the word. It is important to understand that your effectiveness in prayer depends on the level of the word of God in you. I would like you to pay close attention to this scripture: Matthew 6:12 *"Forgive us our debts, AS we forgive our debtors."* The question that I will ask you regarding this statement is: Why should God forgive us? Your answer will be according to this scripture, because we have forgiven. But who asked us to forgive? God is the one telling us to forgive so that we may qualify for his forgiveness. Look at Matthew 6:14 **"For if ye forgive men their trespasses, your heavenly father will also forgive you"**; and Luke 6:37 *"Judge not, and ye shall not be judged: condemn not, and ye shall not be condemned: forgive, and it shall be forgiven"*. We can therefore say of Matthew 6:12 (paraphrase) "Father forgive us, as your word asks us to do." This is simply reminding God of what He has already said. God himself said this very clearly in Isaiah 43:26 *"Put me in remembrance: let us plead together: declare thou, that thou mayest be justified."* (KJV)

The Amplified version says: **"Put me in remembrance [remind me of your merit]; let us plead and argue together. Set forth your case, that you may be justified (proved right)." And the New International version says: "Review the past for me, let us argue the matter together; state the case for your innocence."**

You and I have to defend ourselves according to what is written. Prayer is not a passive, but rather an active action. Your prayer room can be compared to a court room where God is the judge, the devil is the accuser, and you are the defence lawyer.

Notice Jesus' attitude when he was tempted by the devil in Matthew 4:3 to 9. He never cried, screamed or even begged the Father. He simply recalled what was written, as a lawyer will recall what is written in the constitution or the law books.

Verse 4 *"But he answered and said, IT IS WRITTEN…"*.

Verse 7 *"Jesus said unto him IT IS WRITTEN…"* and verse 10 says: *"Then saith Jesus unto him,…, for IT IS WRITTEN"*

Friend, the time has come for you to engage your strongest weapon in God, which is his Word. The situations and circumstances around your life right now cannot match your strength in God. You are a true warrior designed by God, so pull your sword of the spirit (Ephesians 6:17) and cut off the head of that devil. This is the time to declare your freedom. You are the one to defend your case as God says in Isaiah 41:21 *"Produce your cause, saith the Lord; bring forth your strong reasons, saith the King of Jacob."* In the same book of Isaiah 1:18 he says: *"Come now, and let us reason together, saith the Lord: though your sins be as scarlet, they shall be as white as snow; though they be red like crimson, they shall be as wool."*

You cannot afford to go in your prayer room without the adequate word of God and still expect results. This is the fundamental reason why so many people are frustrated in their prayer lives. They use the escape door saying "Maybe it is not the will of God for me to get married, to have children, to have no trouble". If this is you, quit this kind of mentality. The prophet Hosea said in Hosea 14:2: *"Take with you words, and turn to the Lord: SAY UNTO HIM, Take away all iniquity, and receive us graciously..."* Notice in this verse, Hosea is outlining to you and me the fact that we need to SAY. You can only say what you know. We must understand the importance of praying according to the scriptures so that our toiling may no longer be in vain. The time of irresponsible Christianity is over.

Step 5: MAKE YOUR DECLARATION

Matthew 6:13: *"And lead us not into temptation, but deliver us from evil"*

After presenting our strong reasons in accordance with the word of God, it is then important to make a declaration of what we want. Jesus says when you pray, tell the father not to lead you into temptation, but to deliver you from evil, curses, abuses, fornication, cancers, HIV and all kind of infirmities.

Declare what you want. No matter the situation, declare what you want. There is power in any spoken word. God is very committed to what you say. You cannot be going on confessing negativity in your prayer room or outside your prayer room. You may be saying, "But God himself knows my situation. I can't deny my condition." It is true that God knows your situation, but he is not moved by it. Instead, He is committed or moved by what you SAY. God made this very clear in Joel 3:10: *"…let the WEAK [SAY], I am STRONG."* From this scripture you can see that God is aware of your weakness. He is saying, "Do not confess your weakness, but declare your strength." Our father understands the situation, but he is saying do not allow your mouth to confess anything that you do not want.

Remember I said earlier that God knows your situations and problems and he is not moved by them, but rather by what you say. How do I know? Numbers 14:28 says: *"Say unto them, As truly as I live, saith the Lord, as YE HAVE SPOKEN in mine ears, SO WILL I DO TO YOU."* (KJV)

The New American Standard Version says: *"Say to them, 'As I live,' says the Lord, 'JUST AS YOU HAVE SPOKEN in My hearing, so WILL I SURELY DO TO YOU."*

This scripture clearly shows us that the words we say activate the power of God in whichever direction we have engaged them. God is saying to you and me that we reduce his goodness to zero, when we engage our mouth in negative confessions. He says, "I will DO UNTO YOU the very thing I have heard you SAY. Not the very things that you are wishing."

What you say matters a lot in your prayer room, in fact in your life. What are you saying to God? Are you saying: God I understand that this sickness or disease is here to test my faith, but if it is your will let it be so. If this is your kind of prayer, please stop it now.

I pray that God will give you the grace to drop out of the school of negative confession, in Jesus' mighty name.

Jesus said "Tell the Father not to lead you in the way of temptation." It is your choice to either tell the Father or not. Let us stop accusing God of the things that are no longer his responsibility, but ours. The Bible says in Deuteronomy 30:19: *"I call heaven and earth to record this day against you, that I have set before you life and death, blessing and cursing: therefore CHOOSE life, that both thou and thy seed may live."*

Choose what you want. Just declare it. Even if it does not look like it, just say it in order to commit God into action. The words that come out of your mouth have the power to justify or condemn you. According to Matthew 12:36-37: *"But I say unto you, that every idle word that men speak, they shall give account thereof in the day of judgement. For by thy words thou shalt be justified, and by thy words thou shalt be condemned."*

I want you to realise one fundamental truth: every visible and invisible thing is under the power of the spoken word. When God was creating the world, he applied the principle and power of the spoken word. He never cried, neither complained of the fact that there was darkness all over the earth (Genesis Chapter 1, verse 2). All he did was to declare: *"Let there be light."* He spoke the word, *and there was light.*

Your words carry a great amount of power to create or destroy. Remember we were created in the very image of

God. Therefore, we have the full divinity of God working in us.

When God wants to do something, his Word is what he uses. Psalm 107:20 says: **"He sent his WORD, and healed them, and delivered them from their destructions."**

Begin to send words in the area of your life that requires more attention. Stop sitting by and just contemplating your problem. Engage instead, your most powerful weapon, your mouth. Remember what the Bible says in Proverbs 18:21: ***"Death and life are in the power of the tongue: and they that love it shall eat the fruit thereof"***.

Which fruits do you want to eat? Is it the fruit of sorrow, stress, anxiety, etc. I believe your answer is "No", therefore begin to profess your faith through positive declarations against your present challenges.

Do not just repeat "and lead us not into temptation, but deliver us from evil". But instead start working in the revelation of it.

Step 6: HE HAS DONE IT: THANK HIM

Matthew 6:13: *"For thine is the Kingdom, and power, and the glory forever."*

It is important to emphasise at this point that at the end of our prayers, we must again give thanks to God for who He is and for the answer that He has already given. Note that, whenever you give thanks to God for the things that you have not yet seen, what you are doing is expressing your confidence in Him and His Word.

In Jeremiah 29:12 God said: *"Then shall ye call upon me, and ye shall go and pray unto me, and I will hearken unto you."* Hearkening to you and to me is a promise as long as we pray unto Him. Since this is a promise, we can build our confidence on it.

Always take time at the end of your prayer to express your faith to God through thanksgiving. You don't have to wait until you see it, to give Him back the glory. You and I have the confidence according to 1John 5: 14.15: *"And this is the confidence that we have in him, that, if we ask any thing according to his will, he heareth us: And if we know that he hears us, whatsoever we ask, we know that we have the petition that we desired of him."*

It is very important for us to understand that, God is very committed to His Word. His Word is the only thing that justifies His integrity. Whatever His Word says, THAT is what He will do. His Word says that we will have the petition that we desired of Him. Therefore, let us give Him thanks because we know that it is done. The answer has been released from heaven - the manifestation is just a matter of time.

God never lies so give Him thanks. Don't allow the devil to steal the blessing that you have just secured from your prayers, with thoughts like I will really give God thanks when this thing happens. NO, NO, NO. Don't be ignorant! It has already happened, just go ahead and give Him thanks.

The bible goes on presenting in Isaiah 65:24: *"And it shall come to pass, that before they call, I will answer; and while they are yet speaking, I will hear."* This scripture changed my entire view of giving God thanks for the things that I have requested but have not yet seen. Let us give Him thanks, praise and worship, because He is worthy of it all. As you begin to do this, I see God proving Himself in your life in Jesus' name.

Step 7: IN JESUS' NAME

John 14:13.14: *"And whatsoever ye shall ask in my name, that I will do, that my Father may be glorified in the Son. If ye shall ask any thing in my name, I will do it."*

The last step holds the entire power of your prayer. Any time we pray, we must pray in Jesus' name. The reason we must pray in his name is so to remind the Almighty Father of the sacrifice that Christ made for us. When we were in our old sinful nature, we did not have access to the Father; therefore our prayers could not be answered. God had to send his only Son to come and rescue you and me from our sinful state. By sharing His blood, Jesus paid the price for any condemnation that was placed upon us. Not only that, He became the mediator between us and the father. When we pray in his name, we commit Jesus in acting on our behalf, to the Father. This in effect, makes God see us through Christ. All the mistakes and shortcomings of the past, that have been repented, become irrelevant, and cannot stop our prayer.

Always remember to close your prayer with AMEN, which means "let it be so".

PRAYER MODEL

Heavenly father, to you alone be all the glory, honour and praise. I bless your holy name and celebrate who you are. No one is like unto thee. You alone are worthy to be praised and to be worshiped. You are highly lifted up and deserve all the worship from my lips.

I would like to thank you for all that you have done for me and my family. Thank you for protecting us, blessing us, providing for us....

Father, I pray that you may grant me "favour" (replace favour by what you want from him).

For your word say (support your request with biblical scriptures).

Therefore, I declare that divine "favour" (what you ask)is mine. Your favour will speak and announce me where ever I go.

Thank you for your faithfulness. Thank you for hearing and answering my prayer. Take all the glory and praise for the happening.

In Jesus mighty name I have prayed.

Amen

CHAPTER 2

HEARING FROM GOD

Our journey here on earth in pursuit of God's divine plan and purposes for our life, is totally dependent on the voice of God. Anyone who tries to live their life on earth, without being constantly led by God, will be living a life of crisis after crisis.

Understanding and recognising the voice of God is the greatest asset for a successful Christian life. Your fulfilment, attainment and achievement in life, is absolutely dependent on this fact of hearing from God. As mentioned in the introduction, prayer is never complete until you hear back from God concerning your petition.

God is very eager to speak to you. How do I know? He has positioned himself to be your shepherd. We know that a shepherd is a caretaker of sheep. He guides his sheep by sound and corrects them with his rod. Jesus said in John 10:3: *"…and the sheep HEAR his VOICE: and he calleth his own sheep by name, and leadeth them out."* Hearing His voice is God's greatest desire for us. That is why I command your spiritual ear to be opened up in Jesus' precious name. You must desire to hear His voice, because without His voice, you and I will remain helpless in the battle of life.

I believe that David wasn't the strongest or the wisest in Israel. Can we talk about luck? No. Can we talk about the fact that he was God's favourite? No. David had access to the greatest secret of life: THE VOICE OF GOD. All that David did was hearing what God said. Look at this instance, when he returned to Ziklag after assisting Achish. He and his men were very distressed. They were crying because of the disaster that they found. 1 Samuel 30:4.6 says: *"Then David and the people that were with him lifted up their voice and wept, until they had no more power to weep. And David's wives were taken captives, Ahinoam the Jezreelitess, and Abigail the wife of Nabal the Carmelite. And David was greatly distressed; for the people spake of stoning him, because the soul of all the people was grieved, every man for his sons and for his daughters: but David encouraged himself in the Lord his God."* In all of this, what shocks me is the fact that David, knowing that he has never lost a battle, did not run straight to the rescue of his people. Even though his own soldiers wanted to kill him, David didn't move an inch.

I pray that you may not take a step because of the pressure around you, in Jesus' name. Amen.

Right in the middle of all of this, David decided to do what he did best: ENQUIRING from the Lord. 1 Samuel 30:8: *"And David ENQUIRED of the Lord, saying, Shall I pursue after this troops? Shall I overtake them? And HE ANSWERED him, pursue: for thou shall surely overtake them and without fail recovere all."* Things happened exactly has the Lord commanded it.

Another time, in 2 Samuel 2:1, David enquired from the Lord for direction. The Bible says: *"...And the Lord said to him, Go up..."*

In chapter five of the same book of 2nd Samuel, verse 18 to 19, David was confronted by the Philistines. The bible says: *"...and David ENQUIRED of the Lord, ... And the*

Lord said unto David, Go up." Victory was delivered unto him. Yet again, the Philistines came back again in verse 22. I think the right thing for David to have done, was to attack them again. But that is not what he did. In verse 23, he went back to God: *"And when David ENQUIRED of the Lord, HE SAID, Thou shalt not go up; ..."* God gave David a different strategy, and victory was again his.

Let us become addicted to the voice of God. This is our only guarantee for success or promotion in this world.

No one can ever make the most out of anything until they have the correct perspective and understanding of it. This is also true for the VOICE OF GOD. Jesus said in John 10:4: *"And when he putteth forth his own sheep, he goeth before them, and the sheep follow him: for they KNOW HIS VOICE."* This fact of "they know his voice" suggests that there are some characteristics or elements that help identify or differentiate the voice of God from the voice of the stranger (the pretender, the devil).

I would like us to take some time to discover the characteristics and requirements that will help us hear the voice of God constantly.

1- Characteristics of the voice of God

Talking of the characteristic of the voice of God, I would like us to sit at the feet of the prophet Jeremiah the author of the books of Kings (1ˢᵗ and 2ⁿᵈ Kings) to learn about this.

The Bible says in I King 19:10.13: *"And he said, I have been very jealous for the Lord God of hosts: for the children of Israel have forsaken thy covenant, thrown down thine altars, and slain thy prophets with the sword; and I, even I only, am left; and they seek my life, to take it away. And he said, go forth, and stand upon the mount before the Lord. And, behold, the Lord passed by, and a great and strong wind rent the mountains, and brake in pieces the rock before the Lord; but the Lord was not in the wind: and after the wind was an earthquake; but the Lord was not in the earthquake: and after the earthquake was the fire; but the Lord was not in the fire: and after the fire, a still small voice. And it was so, when Elijah heard it, that he wrapped his face in his mantle, and went out, and stood in the entering in of the cave. And, behold, there came a voice unto him, and said, what doest thou here, Elijah?"*

Elijah was a great prophet that God used mightily. Yet even he had a serious problem when he could not hear from God. He even went as far as to ask for death. He asked God to kill him. In verse 4 of chapter 19, of 1 Kings: *"But himself went a day's journey into the wilderness, and came and sat down under a juniper tree: and he requested FOR HIMSELF THAT HE MIGHT DIE; and said, it is enough; now, o Lord TAKE AWAY MY LIFE; for I am not better than my fathers."*

My friend, the voice of God is the only thing that we should desire from now on.

There are four things that I would like us to notice in Elijah's encounter, which were a great and strong wind, the earthquake, the fire and the still small voice. All these characterises something in discerning the voice of God.

a-   Great and strong wind

When the angel told Elijah to stand upon the mount to wait on the Lord so as to hear from him, The Bible says *"…a great and strong wind"* passed, but the Lord was not in it. The great and strong wind could be likened to the voices of our friends and family. The loud voices that we hear are not always the voice of God. Just because your friends tell you that this is the way to go, don't think it is always the voice of God.

Like David, the voices of his soldier were very loud. They ended up entering into him, which at the end caused him to be distress. The people that we talk to the most are our friends and family. Their voices are the ones that remain in us for a long time, in most cases.

Sometime these voices are so strong that they destroy our core beliefs, the standards by which we live our lives. One time, I heard of a sister in Christ that followed the strong wind, considering it to be the voice of God. Her friends told her, *"You know, today's world, you need to be smart. You can't get married without first of all compromising the bed. God knows that we are just human. He will forgive you anyway. There are so many nice men outside the church. Once you find one, give him everything he wants so that you can get married. After that, you can bring him to the church."*

This sister came to me and told me that 'God told her' that her potential husband was an unbelieving brother that I knew very well. When I tried to reason with her, she told me that God had instructed her and I couldn't oppose it. She went further, by threatening to leave the church.

Few weeks later, her 'God-given instruction' became very uncomfortable for her. She couldn't come to me any more for counselling. Why? Because what her God told her could no longer be sustain. God cannot give an instruction and fail you. Everything that God commands always comes to pass. The so called God instruction that the sister had could not be from God, because it went against the total will of God as written in Hebrews 13:4 regarding marriage. You need to know that every voice that you hear from your family members or friends that goes against God's word can never be from God.

Loud voices are not always His voice. Just because someone that goes in the same church as you tells you to do something, doesn't mean that it is the voice of God. The word of God says that the 'wind broke the rock in pieces.' The things that you 'hear' that would seem to break records as far as the realisation of your dreams in terms of time, profit, social status and peer recognition are concerned, are not necessarily the voice of God.

Don't pretend or assume to have heard from God. Make sure it is actually the case. The voice of God is the predominant factor in the school of success.

Your friends, even in the very best of their intention can lead you out of the will of God. Look at Amnon, king David's son. The Bible says that he loved his sister Tamar. He was so vexed, that fell sick for her. The interesting thing here is that the voice of his conscience, which is the place where God talk to us, knew that his feeling for his sister was very wrong. 2 Samuel 13:2 says *"...and Amnon thought it hard for him to do anything to her"*. But it was not long before the voice of his friend and cousin Jonadab changed the basics principle of his life. He told Amnon to pretend to be sick and request that Tamar be sent to take care of him. At this time Amnon did not discern the voice that he was hearing, therefore he ended up raping his sister which led to his greatest fall.

Understand me very well; I am not saying that God cannot speak to you through your friends or family members. The point is that you must discern those voices on the basis of the supreme word of God contained in the book of books call the Bible.

b-   The earthquake

1 Kings 19:11 *"…after the wind an earthquake, but the Lord was not in the earthquake."*

First, I would like to take the time to define the word 'earthquake.' Wikipedia defines it as a "shaking and vibration at the surface of the earth resulting from underground movement along a fault plane of volcanic activity."

The words that drew my attention when checking this definition were: UNDERGROUND MOVEMENT. The earthquake has its origin *under* the ground.

When meditating on this, I asked the Holy Spirit what it was. He revealed to me that the earthquake that he was talking about, were the things that are deep inside of us: OUR DESIRES.

Every desire not properly subdued, represents a serious danger to any faithful Christian. Many times I have heard people say, "God told me" when in reality it was their own desires that were speaking.

Desires have voices. These voices manifest from the inside. Be aware of this fact. Don't pretend to have heard from

God, when all you are doing is fulfilling the desires of your own heart. Don't be moved or controlled by your desires: always keep them under control. I understand that you would like to be successful, but know that God is the only one that guarantees true success. One thing I do know is that no matter what, you will succeed because Jehovah God has planned this from the very beginning. Be patient. Don't allow the desire to marry make you compromise your integrity and respect. Remember, The Bible says in Psalms 127:1-2 *"Except the Lord build the house, they labour in vain that build it: except the Lord keep the city, the watchman waketh but in vain."*

Jehovah God is big enough to defend and beautify your destiny. Any colourful destiny is totally dependent on discerning the voice of God.

Do not sell your destiny for less than what God says it is worth. David refused to be laid by his feelings when he returned to Ziklag. In verse four of chapter thirty of the book of 1st Samuel, The Bible says: *"…then David and the people that were with him lifted up their voice and wept, until they had no more power to weep."*

It is apparent that, being a strong warrior, the best move at the time, would have been to attack the Amalekites. But he didn't.

I believe the reason he did not follow is feelings, is so to avoid Proverbs 14:12 and 16:25 which say: *"there is a way that seemeth right unto a man, but the end thereof are the ways of death"*, to be fulfilled in his life and the lives of his men.

Let me clarify something at this point. I am not trying to say that to desire things from God is demonic or not good. No, no and no. In fact, where there is no desire, there will never be a miracle or manifestation of God's divine power. Jesus said in Mark 11:24: *"...therefore I say unto you, what things so ever ye DESIRE, when ye pray, believe that ye receive them, and ye shall have them."* So to have desires is good, but being overcome or overwhelm by the desires, will always cloud the voice of God.

When Joseph was tempted by Potiphar's wife in Genesis 39:7, he did not give in to that seductive proposition from her. He refused in verse 8 and said in verse 9: *"...how then can I do this great wickedness, and sin against my God?"* Here we can see that the Word of God was the final verdict for Joseph. He didn't allow his *feelings* to have the last word. Don't say "God said" when he has NOT said. Whenever we say "God said" when he did not say, we call judgement upon ourselves. God can never say two different things about the same issue, for he said in Isaiah 55:11: **"So shall my word be that goeth forth out of my mouth: it shall not return unto me void, but it shall accomplish that which I please, and it shall prosper in the thing whereto I sent it."**

One of God's qualities and characteristics is consistency. Allow the Almighty to be the captain of your life. Be a God-driven Christian and not a desire driven Christian only.

c- Fire

After the earthquake, the bible says in I Kings 19:12 that there was a fire. We know that the nature of fire is to burn, to consume everything that comes its way.

The fire here can be likened to your emotions. Wikipedia defines 'emotion' as a "complex psycho-physiological experience of an individual's state of mind as interacting with biochemical (internal) and environmental (external) influences".

From the above definition, your emotions have something to do with your mind. Your mind represents your soul, your centre of reasoning.

Understand this; you are a spirit that has a soul and lives in a body. God is a spirit. Jesus said in John 6:63 "...the WORDS *that I speak unto you, they are SPIRIT and they are life*". Everything that God says will come from the third dimension, which is the realm of the spirit. This will never be of any use, until it is translated by your soul, which in turn will then release it in physical understanding. We can then say that your mind has a very important role to play as far as hearing from God is concerned.

Remember, emotions are dependent on the state of your mind. When your emotions are not controlled, they end up clouding the voice of God. So instead of hearing the voice of God, you start hearing the voice of your emotions. Due to the fact that they have saturated your mind.

It is important for us to know that there are two types of emotions: positive and negative emotion, constructive and destructive emotion. The positive and constructive emotions are enhancers to hearing the voice of God. They always speak the voice of God. However negative and destructive emotions, will never speak the language of God.

Emotions consume like fire. Remember that prophet Elijah was in a very unstable state of mind. He was upset, angry and confused about all that the children of Israel were doing. This was consuming him on the inside. I am certain he was probably hearing a voice - maybe the voice of vengeance. The angel had to intervene and tell Elijah that God was not in the fire (his emotions).

Don't allow the voice of your emotion to take you over. You can't take advantage of people for the sake of becoming rich and say that is 'the voice of God.'

The Bible tells us in 2 Samuel 13:1.14, of the story that we mention earlier of Amnon son of David, who was consumed by his emotions.

Verses one and two say: *"...and it came to pass after this, that Absalom the son of David had a fair sister, whose name was Tamar; and Amnon son of David loved her. And Amnon was so vexed, that he FELL SICK for his sister Tamar; for she was a virgin; and Amnon thought it hard for him to do anything to her."*

Amnon had no control over his emotions, to the point that it began to consume him. He was now sick because of it. In this instance his emotions were like a fire. They were burning everything in him. Clearly this could not have been the voice of God. The voice of God in him could not allow him to do any evil. As The Bible says, he *"thought it hard for him to do anything to her"*. We know that Jehovah was God over Israel and everything was done according to His Word. Despite all of this, because his emotions were not totally controlled, he was still troubled. In verse eleven the bible says: *"and when she (Tamar)brought them unto him to eat, he took hold of her, and said unto her, come and lie with me, my sister."* At this point he could no longer perceive the voice of God, because of the fire burning in his bones. Regardless of the fact that Tamar refused, in verse fourteen the Bible says: *"howbeit he would not hearken unto her voice: but being stronger than she, forced her, and lay with her."* He could not hearken, respond or hear the voice of Tamar, because of the greater voice of his emotions.

Any decision that is made based on negative emotions is not the will of God. For instance, if you pray for God to bless you with a car so that your brother or sister in church may see that God is blessing you, can never be a good foundation to guarantee an answer from God. It's very obvious that, that particular prayer is based on comparison or jealousy. Therefore, hearing the voice of God on what to do or the way that you should take in relation to such a request becomes almost impossible.

Remember again the story of David, when he came to Ziklag and saw what had happened. He didn't take any action or decision in that state of emotional instability. He cooled down his emotions down by comforting himself in the Lord.

Controlling your emotions will help you to constantly hear from God.

d- A still and small voice

1 King 19:12.13 says: *"...and after the fire a STILL AND SMALL VOICE. And it was so, when Elijah heard it, that he wrapped his face in the mantle, and went out, and stood in the entering in of the cave. And, behold, there came a voice unto him, and said, what doest thou here, Elijah?"*

The voice of God is a still and small voice. Halleluiah. This represents his gentleness and majesty. When God speaks, it is with all gentleness and calm. Many people think that the voice of God comes like thunder, as we have seen many times in movies. No.

Jesus said in John 10:4.5: *"... and the sheep follow him: for they know his VOICE. And a stranger will they not follow, but will flee from him: for they know not the voice of strangers."*

It is vital for us to understand this revelation of the main characteristic of the voice of God. God will always speak to you and me. In fact He craves to speak to you every day of your life. He would like to direct every step that you take. The problem that we have is that we are expecting a loud voice that will shout to us.

The stillness of his voice may not always be perceived by your physical ears. He speaks in your heart. In the midst of a situation, always look for that still and small voice.

A loud person cannot hear from God. The loudness that I am talking about here doesn't consist of having a big voice, but the instability of you spirit and soul.

The voice of God is sometimes referred to as the inner voice of a man. It doesn't depend on outward pressures. It is very quiet and relaxed.

From what the Lord Jesus said *"my sheep they know my voice and the voice of the stranger will they not follow"*, I came to the conclusion that there is a way to recognise that voice.

I would like us to appreciate one fundamental truth about His voice. The voice of His Majesty on high, Jehovah God, always speaks peace. Even when he rebukes you, you can still acknowledge that peace in the very inside of you. His voice is never grievous. Whenever you enquire of the Lord, please recognise his voice through the peace that comes with the instruction. Every time you want to do something in the belief that God is the one leading you, but fear is involved, just know that is NOT the voice of God. Fear is the first criteria of the voice of the stranger.

Also the voice of God will never speak anything contrary to His Word. For you to know that the voice you are hearing is really his voice always put it through the test of His Word. Don't tell me that God told you to do something that is totally opposed to his Word.

At the very beginning of our ministry in London, I was confronted with a situation that really made me laugh. There was a brother that approached me asking me to agree with him in prayer concerning marriage. I asked him to tell me a bit about it.

The first thing he told me was that God told him about a certain sister that was going to be his wife. So I asked him about the sister. He told me that she was married, but that God had told him that the man was not her husband, but he was. I asked him what the sister thought about what 'God' had told him. Apparently, she did not agree and was not interested in him. But he believed that was a distraction from the devil and therefore we needed to fast and pray about it.

Straight away, I could tell that this was not the voice of God that he heard, but the voice of his emotions, the fire. What he said was the voice of God, did not agree with the Word of God. The Word of God says that marriage is an agreement. It says in Proverbs 18:22: *"whoso, findeth a wife findeth a good thing, and obtaineth favour of the Lord."* The word finding represents the agreement that needs to take place between the two parties involved. On that basis, I told the brother that the 'voice' he heard, could not have been God. He became upset and left the church. A few years later, I ask him about the sister, he told me that 'God' had given him another direction, which was to marry another woman who is his present wife. Remember, God will never say two different things about the same issue. He can never repent or change what He says - Psalm 89:34: *"My covenant will I not break, nor alter the thing that is gone out of my lips"* and 2 Timothy 2:13: *"If we believe not, yet He (God) abideth faithful: He cannot deny himself"*.

For instance in the area of business, you can't be going around bribing people to get business contracts, in the name of 'the voice of God', for the Bible says in Psalms 33:4: *"For the word of the Lord is right; and all his works are done in truth."*

I pray that you may always recognise and keep on walking according to the voice of God. Do not pretend that God spoke to you when all you are doing is going against his word. The word of God is the final verdict, the final test of his voice.

2- Atmosphere required to hear from God

It is important for us to note and consider at this point that, the fact that the voice of God is still and small, an appropriate atmosphere is required in order for us to recognise it. The atmosphere required is "QUIETNESS". This can be divided into two states:

The internal quietness: the quietness in your spirit and soul.

And

The external quietness: the environment in which you are.

a- Internal quietness

The internal quietness relates to the tranquillity that needs to be or take place in the inner part of your being. The louder you are internally, the more sure you are to miss his voice. The noises that take place in your inner being are represented by anxiety, tension, stress, sorrow and so on.

Jesus said in Matthew 6:6: *"...when thou prayest, enter into thy closet, and when thou hast SHUT THE DOOR, pray to thy father...".* Shutting the door can be perceived in two dimensions; the physical door and the spiritual door, which is your mind. So the Lord is saying, don't go in your prayer room under the pressure of your situation. In order words, don't allow the pressure and tension to get inside you.

Let me clarify this point. I am not saying that you cannot pray when you are confronted with some fierce challenges. But rather, don't allow the negative effect of the situation to crystallise on the inside of you. Anxiety is the proof that your situation has entered and settled in the inside of you.

The internal quietness is one of the greatest assets in the 'school of the voice of God.' The Bible says in 1 Peter 3:4: *"... let it be the hidden man of the heart, in that which is not corruptible, even the ornament of a meek and QUIET SPIRIT, which is in the sight of God of GREAT PRICE".*

You must create this internal quietness. Your success in discerning the voice of God depends on it. The internal quietness facilitates your access to his voice. The quieter you are, the clearer his voice becomes.

The Master, Jesus, any time he faced a challenging situation or had a confrontation with the scribes, would always create the internal peace to know what God was saying regarding the situation. He demonstrated this on several occasions. For example, when he was confronted with regards to the woman that committed adultery, the Bible says in John 8:6: "*... Jesus stooped down, and with his finger wrote on the ground, as though HE HEARD THEM NOT*". Why did it look as if he did not hear them? Simply because he needed to create an internal quietness so that he could connect to the heavenly source.

We need to appreciate the vitality of this factor if we want to enjoy the best of God in life and ministry. Let us create and maintain this internal quietness. The Lord Jesus Christ repeated on several occasions the need for us not to be troubled, in other words to always maintains the internal quietness. He said in Matthew chapter 6 and verse 25 "*... take no thought for your life*".

Verse 27 "*...which of you by taking thought can add one cubit unto his stature?*"

Verse 28 "*Why take ye thought for raiment?*"

Verse 31 "*...take no thought...*"

Verse 34 "*...take therefore no thought...*"

Luke 12:22 *"...take no thought for your life..."*

And the list goes on.

This doesn't mean that we should not think or plan for our future and our life. All He is saying is: do not permit negative emotions to grow inside you. Even when it looks like there is nothing to eat, know that the God who feeds the birds, will provide for you.

The devil has no power over you. He can neither destroy you, nor anything that belongs to you. He knows that he will forever remain helpless as long as you are walking in the path of God. All he does is to try and create distractions that will break your concentration in hearing from God. Once this is done, you will start having difficulties discerning the next step of God's plan for your life. Isaiah the prophet said in Isaiah 30:15: *"For thus saith the Lord God, the Holy one of Israel; In returning and rest shall ye be saved; in QUIETNESS and in confidence shall be your strength ..."* Your spiritual strength depends on this.

Take charge of your life by developing this ability. You have to be practically and totally involved in the building up of this ability. It will not just happen.

The internal quietness is a fertile ground for the Holy Spirit to minister unto our spirit, soul and body.

Jesus was addicted to this. The question I asked myself was, why? I discovered the answer in John 5:30: *"I can of my own self do nothing: as I HEAR, I JUDGE: and my judgement is JUST..."*

Why was His judgement always right? Because of what he heard, that came from God.

Every day and night, check the conversation that goes on the inside of you. Any 'loud' conversations: unbelief, fear of the future, doubts, etc, must not be allowed to take place. No matter the circumstances, always know that God knows best, therefore you should not be troubled. He has your best interests in heart. He always works behind the scenes. It is just a matter of time before you manifest God's reality.

The bible tells us in Exodus 14:9.10, that after the departure of the children of Israel from Egypt: *"...the Egyptians pursued after them, all the horses and chariots of Pharaoh, and his horsemen, and his army, and overtook them encamping by the sea, beside Pihahiroth, before Baal-zephon. And when Pharaoh drew nigh, the children of Israel lifted up their EYES, and behold, the Egyptians marched after them; and so were sore AFRAID: and the children of Israel cried out unto the Lord".* Notice here, the children of Israel first of all saw the Egyptians approaching, and that picture created fear in them. But the interesting thing is that God did not permit them to dwell under the spirit of fear. So in verse 13, He said *"... fear not, stand still, and see the salvation of the Lord, which he will shew to you today: the Egyptians whom ye have seen today, ye shall see them again no more forever."*

Jehovah had to stop them first from fearing, so that they could enjoy His backing, which was only guaranteed through His leading, which comes through His voice. If the Lord had not stopped that negative internal dialogue, fear, they would not have been able to distinguish his voice.

b- External quietness

As much as internal quietness is important, so also is external quietness. The atmosphere that you create around you, determines the experience that you have. Creating an environment of quietness is essential, because it will help your concentration in hearing, discerning and understanding the voice of God.

Remember, the voice of God is a still and small voice. A noisy environment will never be conducive to discern His voice. We need to take some time to create quietness around us.

The Lord Jesus Christ taught us this by personal example. The bible says in:

Luke 4:42 *"and when it was day, he departed and went into a desert place…"*

Luke 5:16 *"And he withdrew himself into the wilderness, and prayed."*

Luke 6:12 *"And it came to pass in those days, that he went out into a mountain to pray, and continued all night in prayer to God."*

Mark 1:35 *"And in the morning, rising up a great while before day, he went out, and departed into a solitary place, and there prayed."*

Mark 6:46 *"And when he had sent them away, he departed into a mountain to pray."*

Matthew 14:23 *"And when he had sent the multitudes away, he went up into a mountain apart to pray: and when the evening was come, he was there alone."*

And the scriptural references go on.

We can see from the references above that environmental quietness was a very important part of the Master's prayer life. Whenever he wanted to connect himself with the heavenly Source, he always went into a quiet place.

One of my most respected mentors, **Dr Al Baxter** of the Faith Miracle Temple Toronto, always says "The quality of the environmental quietness in which you live, determines the quality of any mental product that you produce".

This is so true. I remember when I was preparing my degree in Accountancy and Finance. I would spend hours and hours in the library studying. In the library there was a place that was clearly marked "Quiet Area". No phones or talking were allowed. It was so peaceful and nice to study there. Whenever I was in that environment, I wished that the library could always stay open. Why? Because the pace at which I absorbed the subject of the day was phenomenal.

Your environment plays a great part in being able to access the things of God. A negative environment for instance, will affect your spirit of faith. We know that without faith it is impossible to please God (Hebrews 11:6). It is important for us to understand that the environment that we are referring to here is not only about the place, but also about the people that surround you when you are in your secret place with God. You cannot afford to have people that have a negative spirit, in ANY aspect of your life.

Notice this: when Jesus was invited to pray for the young girl in Matthew chapter 9 from verse 18 to 19, The Bible says: *"While he spake these things unto them, behold, there came a certain ruler, and worshipped him, saying, my daughter is even now dead: but come and lay thy hand upon her, and she shall live. And Jesus arose, and followed him..."*

And verse 23 to 25 say: *"And when Jesus came into the ruler's house, and saw the minstrels and the people making a noise, he said unto them, give place for the maid is not dead, but sleepeth. And they laughed him to scorn. But when the people were put forth, he went in and took her by the hand, and the maid arose."*

I believe that if the people were not taken out of the room, Jesus would not have been able to reach the maid and save her from the spirit of death. They had to clear the room first, so that he could come in and perform the miracle.

The atmosphere you create around you is the principal element that determines the manifestation of the expected miracle. A quiet environment helps break the spirit of distraction. Your concentration, which is enhanced by a quiet environment, has a great value in the eyes of God.

The divine encounter that took place in the life of Jacob that led to the change of his name, was favoured by a quiet environment. The bible says in Genesis 32:24: **"And Jacob was left ALONE; and there wrestled a man with him until the breaking of the day."** Until he was left alone, he couldn't reason as to what to do once in front of his brother. The act of reasoning is simply the act of meditation. Perfect meditation is totally dependent on the silence around you. God believes in meditation (reasoning with God), that's why he said in Isaiah 1:18: **"Come now, and let us reason together, saith the Lord…"**.

3- The prerequisite to hear from God

Hearing, discerning, recognising and understanding the voice of God is so vital for a successful Christian life, as we have seen in the previous line of this book.

It is essential for us to note that there are some prerequisites that need to be in place before we can ever enjoy the voice of God. Once these things are established, the voice of God becomes part of our daily life.

a- BE BORN AGAIN

John 10:3.5 *"...the SHEEP hear his voice: and he calleth HIS OWN SHEEP by name, and leadeth them out. And when he putteth forth HIS OWN SHEEP, he goeth before them, and the sheep follow him: for they KNOW his voice. And a stranger will they not follow, but will flee from him: for they know not the voice of the strangers."*

A close reading of these scriptures brings out a particular and specific word of difference that God makes towards every man and woman living on this earth. He makes a difference between HIS OWN and those that are not his own. He says his sheep know his voice. In other words, they recognise his voice. They can clearly discern the voice of the stranger, from the voice of the master.

From this explanation, we therefore come to understand that hearing the voice of God begins with you and me becoming his sheep. This is also known as being born again.

Being born again consists of rejecting our old (sinful, disobedient) nature and embracing the nature of God, by accepting Jesus Christ as our personal Lord and Saviour.

We need to appreciate the fact that God leads only his sheep. The bible says in the book of Psalms 23:1: *"The Lord is my shepherd; I shall not want."* Until you make him your shepherd, you will always want.

Being born again is the first step of Christianity. You can't *guess* whether you are born again or not. You must be sure. It is not optional, but compulsory. No revelation of the Word or ways of God can be accessed without it.

Jesus was approached one night by Nicodemus. Nicodemus was a Pharisee, a ruler of the Jews. He was among the law-makers, those that represented the totality of the law. The reason he came to Jesus was because of the wisdom and depth of revelation that he displayed of the Word of God.

He said in John 3:2: *"... Rabbi, we know that thou art a teacher come from God: for no man can do these miracles that thou doest, except God be with him."*

The astonishing thing here was the answer that came from Jesus. In verse 3 The Bible says: **"Jesus answered and said unto him. Verily, verily, I say unto thee, Except a man BE BORN AGAIN, he cannot see the kingdom of God."** The kingdom of God simply means, the ways of God.

In verse 7 The Bible goes on, saying: *"Marvel not that I said unto thee, ye MUST be born again."* As I said earlier, everything begins here, and it is compulsory.

Jesus was sent into the world for the redemption of your spirit, soul and body. He died for us so that through his death we might come alive. When you accept Jesus Christ as your Lord and Saviour, all you are doing is expressing your faith that he is the Christ that came and died for you. As a result of that, you are born again. The Bible testifies to this in 1 John 5:1: *"...whosoever believeth that Jesus is the Christ, is born of God".* When you do this, you activate the power in John 3:16 that says: *"...that whosoever believeth in him should not PERISH, but have EVERLASTING LIFE."*

You must first be alive to talk of hearing from God. New birth is the process designed by Jehovah God, to bring us back to life. It is the fundamental and principle fact of Christianity. It translates you from carnality to divinity.

Remember, Jesus says if you are not born again you cannot see the kingdom of God. In other words, if you are not born again, you cannot understand the ways and things of God. God said in Isaiah 55:9: *"For as the heavens are higher than the earth, so are my ways higher than your ways, and my thoughts than your thoughts."*

It takes a regenerated spirit to comprehend the things of God. You can't enjoy the true bounties of God until you are born again. You will forever remain a stranger in the sight of God, until you receive Jesus Christ in your life by confessing him as your Lord and saviour. It doesn't matter how far you have gone away from him, or how many things you have done wrong in your life. By acknowledging him in your life, he will wipe away all your reproach and sins, which are all blocks when it comes to discerning the voice of God.

b- FEAR OF THE LORD

Proverbs 1:7 *"The FEAR OF THE LORD is the beginning of knowledge: but fools despise wisdom and instruction."*

The knowledge of God is the foundation of true strength and great performance of exploits, as The Bible says in the book of Daniel 11:32: *"…but the people that do KNOW their God shall be strong, and do exploits."*

We read in Proverbs 1:7 that knowledge has a beginning, and its beginning is the fear of the Lord. Therefore understanding the FEAR OF THE LORD becomes something of very great importance.

Before exploring this, I would like us to grasp the basic understanding of the fear of the Lord. This does not consist of trembling in front of God or of being scared of him. The fear of the Lord represents our *profound reverence, admiration, respect and awe toward God.*

No one can ever enjoy the constant hearing of the voice of God, until the fear of the Lord is in their heart.

The bible says in Psalm 34:9: *"O fear the Lord, ye his saints: for there is no want to them that fear him."* This scripture confirms that the fear of the Lord is the guaranteed element for stability in any life, because it forbids lack and want. We need to understand deep inside of ourselves that the fear of the Lord in our heart determines the limits of our accomplishment.

The fear of the Lord is not characterised by the holy look that some may put on. It is not dependent on the outside appearance, but is an inner quality. It comes from the heart. True reverence speaks thousands of miles away from the person in question. We do not prove this fear only on Sunday when we go to church, neither when we go into our prayer room. Instead it should be a way of life.

I believe that every attainment in life has everything to do with the fear of Lord. The undeniable help of God in the life of Joseph, was a clear result of his respect toward God and his instruction. Remember Joseph in the house of Potiphar. He had all authority and control over everything that belonged to his master. In other words, he was equal to his master as far as managing the business of Potiphar was concerned. There was one thing that was not given to him by his master, which was his master's wife. One day Joseph was approached by his master's wife asking him to come and lie with her. This was an opportunity for him to finally become totally equal to Potiphar by sharing the same woman. Remember that they were left alone, so this would have been a secret between the two of them. But because of the true fear of God in his heart, Joseph answered her in Genesis 39:8.9: *"…behold, my master wotteth not what is with me in the house, and hath committed all that he hath in my hand; there is none greater in this house than I; neither hath he kept back any thing from me but thee, because thou art his wife: how then can I do this great wickedness, and SIN AGAINST MY GOD?"*

From this response, it is apparent that God was at the centre of Joseph's morality, consciousness and personality. Everything Joseph did, he always weighed it in the balance of God.

Let us stop faking this. It is not what we say in front of people that will impress God. It is what we do when all eyes are closed. That's why Hannah advises us in 1 Samuel 2:3 that we should *"talk no more so exceeding proudly; let no arrogance come out of your mouth; for the Lord is a God of knowledge, and by him, our ACTIONS ARE WEIGHED."*

My dear brother and sister let us fear the Lord. Let us reverence him and admire him in all his form and personality. **Dr Mike Murdock** once said "The anointing you respect, is the anointing that you will attract". Until true respect is given to Jehovah God, we can never expect the best of him. The fear of the Lord is a double-edged sword. It secures God's presence and guarantees his blessing upon us. The Bible says in Psalm 112:1.3 *"...blessed is the man that feareth the Lord,...His seed shall be mighty upon earth...wealth and riches shall be in his house..."* One day the Lord told me that the blessing of a man that fears the Lord, always outlive him. As verse 2 of Psalm 112 says, *"...the generation of the upright shall be blessed".* We can see that the fear of the Lord does not affect only the life of the person that fears the Lord. Look at Noah, Abraham, Isaac, Jacob and Joseph. The fear of the Lord in their hearts caused them to be great blessings to their generation and beyond.

The fear of the Lord is a must. Everyone should work on this inner virtue. The wisdom of God upon you depends on it.

Proverbs 15:33: **"...the fear of the Lord is the instruction of wisdom".** I pray that God may empower you for total reverence of His person in the precious name of Jesus.

c- FAITH

Hebrews 11:6: *"But without faith it is impossible to please him: for he that cometh to God MUST BELIEVE that he is, and that he is a rewarder of them that diligently seek him."*

Faith is also a compulsory thing as being born again is. In this Kingdom in which we live, absolutely nothing can be done without it. No one can access, hear or understand the voice of God without faith. The Bible defines faith in Hebrews 11:1: as *"...the substance of things hoped for, the evidence of things not seen."* In other words, faith is the act of behaving as though we have something, that we do not yet physical hold.

One day during a Bible study in church, the Holy Spirit helped me understand this element of faith, by defining it in another way. He said, 'Faith is *the fact of being conscious of the ability of God in getting things done.*'

Faith is fundamental for a successful Christian life. There is nothing that can be done in our Christian walk without it. No one can ever please God without faith. How far you get in life, is determined by it. Faith is the blood of every achievement in God. We can never comprehend the wisdom, the ways of God without it.

It is almost impossible to discern the voice of God without faith. Remember that the ways of God are higher than our ways and his thoughts deeper than our thoughts. God always speaks out of time and circumstances. Often, what he says won't match your present situation. It is only faith that will be able to recognise the voice of God.

There is no Christianity without faith. No one can obtain anything from God without the force of faith. You need to understand that until your faith in God is in place, you can never have a future of distinction on earth.

The Bible testifies that Abel, Enoch, Noah, Abraham, Sarah, Isaac, Jacob, Joseph, Moses, Gideon, Barak, Samson, Jephthae, David, Samuel and the prophets, all made it by faith.

Faith is believing that what God said is what will happen, and therefore behave like it. Faith is not a feeling, neither a philosophy. It is not a mental concept. Faith is never made perfect until a corresponding action is undertaken in relation to the thing that you are believing God for. Paul say in James 2:17.18: *"Even so faith, if it hath not works, is dead, being alone. Yea, a man may say, thou hast faith, and I have works: shew me thy faith without thy works, and I will shew thee my faith by my works"*. Until your faith has works, practical action it will remain fruitless. God is not impressed by the fact that you are saying that I have faith. But, he is impressed when you take action backing up what you say.

d- HUMILITY

Humility can be defined as the act of being humble. To be humble is not having any pride or arrogance, having a spirit of submission or deference or to bring into submission.

Without humility no one can hear or be led by God. A humble spirit is one that accepts correction. All divine corrections are aimed at the ultimate glorification of the one being corrected. Only fools hate correction. I always say 'Humility is the ticket to greatness'. You can never see God's glory or honour without it. The Bible says in the book

of Proverbs 15:33 and 18:12 *"...before honour is humility."*
The type of honour you can enjoy depends on your level of
humility. Be humble. A proud spirit blocks your spiritual
ears. When you are proud, you become too loud for the
voice of God. Humility enhances your spiritual capacity.

A proud person always sees himself as the doer and maker
of his or her life. As well as the fear of the Lord, this is
a virtue of the heart. Humility has a presence. You can
tell whether someone is humble or proud. One day I was
speaking with one of my daughters in the Lord over the
phone, and she said 'I can't control my tears when I speak
with you, because I can feel the spirit of humility in you.'

Friends, you don't talk humility, but you live it and you are
it. A proud spirit cannot stand the presence of the Lord.
You cannot hear from Him unless you have a meek spirit.
The Bible says in Psalm 25:9: *"the MEEK will He guide
in judgement: and the MEEK will He teach His way."*
From this passage, I am sure you can see the importance
of meekness. You cannot access His ways and He cannot
teach you His ways, if you are not meek. We know that
his ways are higher than our ways. Your potential remains
dormant until the force of humility is engaged. Be humble.

This is not something to possess, but it is something you MUST BE.

The unusual backing and defence that Moses experienced from God was a result of his humble spirit. The Bible testifies of him in Number 12:3 *"Now the man Moses was very meek, above all the men which were upon the face of the earth".* When Aaron and Miriam tried to backstab Moses because of his humble spirit, God defended him by plaguing Miriam with leprosy.

You can never go wrong when you are humble. The humble spirit of Moses made him gain unusual access to God. God said in Numbers 12:8: *"…with him will I speak mouth to mouth".* Every step Moses took was directly commanded by God.

Zephaniah 2:3: *"Seek the Lord, all ye meek of the earth, which have wrought his judgement; seek righteousness, SEEK MEEKNESS: it may be ye shall be hid in the day of the Lord's anger."*

This scripture make us understand that righteousness and humility, meekness do not just happen. They are things that we must seek. They must be consciously cultivated. We have to be practically and totally involved in the acquisition of these virtues. He says, SEEK MEEKNESS. How? Through prayer and careful study of His will. But most importantly, you must have a desperate, longing, deep desire, to become it.

Remember, meekness is not the appearance that you put out there, but it is the perfect response to every demand of the scripture. Receive now the spirit of meekness in Jesus' name.

The meek will He guide. They thirsted not when He led them through the desert (Isaiah 48:21). You can never walk with God, nor resist the devil without humility. The Bible says in James 4:7: *"Submit yourselves therefore to God. Resist the devil, and he will flee from you."*

The divine empowerment to resist starts with you submitting to God. Until you are totally submitted to God (the demand of the scriptures) the strength to resist will never be there. Why? Because you will be void of his presence.

No one can make it in this life or walk with God without it. Make it your priority today. You must crave for it. Meekness pays a great dividend to whoever invests in it.

e- TOTAL DEPENDENCY

Jeremiah 17:7.8: *"Blessed is the man that trusteth in the Lord, and whose hope the Lord is. For he shall be as a tree planted by the waters, and that spreadeth out her roots by the river, and shall not see when heat cometh, but her leaf shall be green; and shall not be careful in the year of drought, neither shall cease from yielding fruit."*

This picture helps us see the fruits of total dependency on God. You can't be totally dependent on God and live a wasted life on earth. Total dependency on God commits the entire heavens to your case. A man that is totally depending on God attracts the attention of God.

You cannot be properly led by God until you are totally dependent on him. Depending totally on God means that you hold God's Word to you as the only viable and adequate truth of your life.

The reality is this; life has some fierce challenges that sometimes make us doubt the promises of God. I don't know what you are going through right now. Maybe you are about to lose your house or your car. Maybe your marriage is in deep trouble. I want you to know that you can still depend on Him. Remember, the scripture says, *"Blessed* is the man that trusteth in the Lord." You guarantee the blessings of God in your life, by trusting in Him.

To fly on the high wings of life, your trust must be totally secured.

There is a common saying that goes on like: *"It is the people that you know that will determine what you become in life."* This is a total lie from the pit of hell. If you are someone who believes this to be true, I want you to know that the devil is simply trying to break your trust in God, by shifting it to the trust of man.

The Bible tells me still in the same book of Jeremiah 17:5.6 that: ***"Thus saith the Lord; Cursed be the man that trusteth in man, and maketh flesh his arm, and whose heart departeth from the Lord. For he shall be like a heath in the desert, and shall not see when good cometh; but shall inhabit the parched places in the wilderness, in a salt land and not inhabited."***

You place yourself under a curse that no one can deliver you from, when you put your trust into men. Any help from man is vain. Abraham was dangerously blessed by God, because he proved his totally dependency on God many times.

Look at this; Abraham had a promise from God that he was going to bless him and make him a blessing, in Genesis 12:2.3. That was wonderful. Let me say this, between the promise and its accomplishment, there is a period of testing. God will first prove you before presenting you to your world (1 Samuel 2:3). There is a world that has been prepared for you from creation so that you may display the glory of God, most importantly for you to shine and manifest. You are a role model for someone out there.

As I said earlier, although Abraham had the promise, he needed to prove that he was totally dependent on God.

Genesis 14:21.23 says: *"And the King of Sodom said unto Abram, 'Give me the persons, and take the goods to thyself.' And Abram said to the King of Sodom, 'I HAVE LIFT UP MINE HAND UNTO THE LORD, THE MOST HIGH GOD, THE POSSESSOR OF HEAVEN AND EARTH. That I WILL NOT TAKE from thee even a shoelatchet, and that I WILL NOT TAKE ANY THING THAT IS THINE, lest thou shouldest say, "I have made Abram rich."*

The day I had the revelation of this scripture, I shouted and was totally shaken by it. Notice this: Abram had an opportunity to become rich, for this is the promise that God gave him. Yet when he perceived that it was not God, he automatically rejected it. I am sure he had the understanding of Jeremiah 17:11 that says: *"…he that getteth riches, and not by right, shall leave them in the midst of his days, and at his end shall be a fool."*

What he did rather, was to declare his total dependency on God by saying: "I have lift up mine hand unto the Lord, the most high God, the possessor of heaven and earth…I will not take anything that is thine." Listen to God's response after this public declaration of Abram's totally dependency, in Genesis 15:1 *"After these things the Word of the Lord came unto Abram in a vision, saying, 'Fear not, Abram: I am thy shield, and thy exceeding great reward'."*

Clearly, after that public declaration, Abram's words provoked God. He had no choice but to tell him that his (God's) materials blessings were too small to be his reward. God himself became Abram's reward.

The realisation of any dream depends on this. Decide today to totally depend on God.

Another time, God came back to check the truth about Abraham. Genesis 22:1.2 says: *"And it came to pass after these things, that God did tempt Abraham, and said unto him, 'Abraham': And he said, 'behold, here I am.' And he said, 'Take now thy son, thine only son Isaac, whom thou lovest, and get thee into the land of Moriah; and offer him there for a burnt offering upon one of the mountains which I will tell thee of'."*

Until you are totally proven by God, you can never qualify for greater manifestation. I always say, do not envy or be jealous of your brother or sister's blessings. Do not try to understand how God did that for them, but rather, try to know and understand their level of dependency on God.

Isaac was the only legitimate son of Abraham. How fair could this one be, for God to come and ask him for the only thing he had? From the human perception, this was not at all fair. Abraham's addiction to total dependency on God, made him obey without question or a second thought. Verse 3 says, *"And Abraham rose up early in the morning"*. Let us pause for a moment. Try to imagine that night for Abraham. Yet early in morning he rose, suggesting that he saw God's demand as mandatory for the divine accomplishment in his life. In other words, he trusted God in everything. I am sure Abraham must have considered his age, his wife's age, so on, but he still came to the decision that God was right. Imagine his pain as he walked towards that mountain.

Total dependency is proven by your trust. Trust is proven by your total obedience. 'Half' obedience is disobedience. I always say that Abraham killed Isaac. You may say 'How?' In his heart. Abraham never considered stopping until God told him to stop. He trusted God so much that the bible says in verse 10, *"And Abraham stretched forth his hand, and took the knife to slay his son"*. For him it was a done deal, because God had commanded it. It took God to stop him. My friend, I dare you to depend on this God.

When God saw that Abraham's trust towards him had no limit, He was short of words. He did not know what to say, what words he could use to guarantee him His blessings. He had no choice but to use his heavy 'weapon', which is his name. In verses 16 to 18 of chapter 22 of Genesis, God said: *"... BY MYSELF HAVE I SWORN, saith the Lord, for because thou hast done this thing, and hast not withheld thy son, thine only one: that in blessing I will bless thee, and in multiplying I will multiply thy seed as the stars of the heaven, and as the sand which is upon the sea shore; and your seed shall possess the gate of his enemies; And in thy seed shall all the nations of the earth be blessed; because thou hast OBEYED MY VOICE."* I say halleluiah to Jehovah God, the reliable, dependable, believable and trustworthy God.

Know this, your dependency on God is a process through which a spiritual transfer of your problems and challenges are made to God, so that He may change any stress to rejoicing, any curses into blessings.

I deeply believe that David also had the understanding of a total dependency on God. David said in Psalm 63:8, *"My soul followeth hard after thee: thy right hand upholdeth me."* My understanding is that you cannot follow someone that you don't trust, and remember that trust is the proof of total dependency on God.

Again, choose to be totally dependent on Him today in Jesus' name.

A FINAL WORD

Before I conclude this book, understand that all the knowledge and revelation that you have acquire will not profit you until you have made Jesus Christ the Lord and saviour of your life. As we have seen in the previous lines, been born again is a MUST.

Therefore, if you are not or are not sure that you are born again, or may be have gone back to your old ways, I would like you to repeat this prayer after me.

Lord Jesus, I come to You today.

I am a sinner, I cannot help myself.

Forgive me my sin. Cleanse me with your precious blood.

Deliver me from sin and Satan, to serve the living God.

I renounce any covenant that I have made that do not glorify your name.

Today, Lord Jesus, I accept you as my Lord and my Saviour.

Thank you Jesus, for saving me! Now I declare that I am born again.

Amen

BOOK ENCOUNTER

I believe this book has been a blessing to you and has ushered you into a new realm of understanding with signs and wonder.

I will be looking forward to hearing what the Lord has done for you through the encounter that you have had in this book.

Visit our website for more products.

Write or call us on:

VICTORY CHAPEL
46 Chaffinch way,
Newport, NP10 8WQ
South Wales

Tel: (0044)1633 817589
Fax: (0044)1633 817590
www.vcicuk.com
www.victoryinlondon.wordpress.com

ABOUT THE AUTHOR

Pastor Joseph Dosso is a dynamic international preacher who has gone through the spiritual elements of wind, rain and flood. His ability to keep standing is the result of a God given special anointing. As a mentor to Joseph I have watch him grown into a stalwart and powerful man of God, with a formidable healing ministry. Pastor Joseph has paid the price through being ridiculed, reviled, rejected and even abused, sometimes by those who he loved and trusted. Pastor Joseph has earned the respect of those who know him. He has accomplished his degrees in Accounting and Finance at the University of Wales, Newport (UWN) and is currently seeking to acquire his doctoral degree in divinity. He is married to a beautiful lady name Marie Louise. God has blessed them with three precious and wonderful children: Pascaline, Daniel Joseph and Charlotte.